Watersong

Watersong

Andy Brown

Shearsman Books

First published in the United Kingdom in 2015 by
Shearsman Books
50 Westons Hill Drive
Emersons Green
BRISTOL
BS16 7DF

Shearsman Books Ltd Registered Office
30–31 St. James Place, Mangotsfield, Bristol BS16 9JB
(this address not for correspondence)

www.shearsman.com

ISBN 978-1-84861-450-5

Copyright © Andy Brown, 2015

The right of Andy Brown to be identified as the author of this work has been asserted by him in accordance with the Copyrights, Designs and Patents Act of 1988. All rights reserved.

Acknowledgements

Special thanks are due to Professor Mark Jackson and Exeter University's HASS Strategy, for the funding to initiate a research project concerning poetry, water and sanitation, and for the time and support to research and write these poems alongside other related critical and edited works.

Contents

Watersong	7
The Unnameable Taxonomy	24
The Broad Street Pump	26
The G7 Aid Budget	27
The Flying Toilets of Kibera	28
Notes	30

Watersong

*A great plague of pestilence enterd this citie,
chiefly occasiond through unforeseen heat.
The citie by affliction is left barren.*
    Plague. Plague. Plague. Plague. Plague.

*The citie quarantind v. London goods.
The fayre by St Nicholas cancelld.
Citie leaders ryding for the countrie.*
    Plague. Plague. Plague. Plague. Plague.

*Prisoners expire from sweating sickness –
with likenesses to* cholera nostrum,
*glandular and petechial
plague.* Plague. Plague. Plague. Plague.

•

Where open gutters run with household slops
and muck, the public hasten. No one stops.

•

Against the Widow Knot, for a house of office
emptying over the King's high way, amerced 2l. 6s.
The Widow Barrier, for a nucence by keeping a mound
of filth and nastiness beneath her court, amerced 5l. 8s.

From Solomon Humbleby, for refusing the party vault
to be emptied thro' his property, amerced 10s. 4d.
Christopher Scrape, for throwing out nightsoile
and sundry muck into the street, amerced 5s. 8d.

Against John Tinckler, for making a dung wharffe and laystall,
and laying there the dung of severall parishes
to the damage and nucence of all, amerced 5l.

From Josiah Jarvis, for annoying his neighbour
by throwing out filth and soile, and for an insult
to the jury effecting their office, amerced 10l.

•

On July 23rd, at Pester Lane –
the son of a journeyman bricklayer.
Cholera 4 days. A crowded row of houses;
no drainage for those who live within,
save for a small tub sunk into the earth;
waste water carried out by hand
and thrown into the gutter of the street.

On July 24th, at Bury Lane –
the wife of a journeyman cordwainer.
Cholera 3 days. A crowded, ill-cleans'd,
undrain'd street, adjoining the churchyard.
No public sewer and drainage
of no very perfect principle.

On July 27th, at Bartholomew Street –
the girl of a journeyman housepainter.
Cholera 5 days. An ill-cleans'd lane
with rank and undrain'd cobbles.
The narrow street both close and airless,
unfavourable to public health.

On August 1st, at Butcher's Row –
a journeyman butcher. Cholera 24 hours.
This dwelling house a home to fifteen families.
Dungheaps prevalent, pigs and poultry
in the yard, with others also slaughtered here,
their offal thrown out in between.

On August 3rd, at Bridge Street, Exe Island –
nightsoil man. Cholera 48 hours.
The third death in the same household,
occasion'd by fright upon seeing a coffin
carried underhand to interment.

•

The surgeon in his frock coat and bow tie
inserts his hands inside the opened skull
to find the brain within is coarse and dry.

Beneath the ribs, the pleura are quite healthy,
but both lungs are engorged with blackened blood.
The same is true of both the poor and wealthy.

His scalpel slices through the muscle wall.
The stomach and intestines both distended;
the bladder filled with vitiated gall.

The bowel empty now of gruel dejections;
the urinary bladder greatly shrunk
in each and every one of his inspections.

Before the opened torso is sewn closed
he strokes the black heart – 'Flabby', *'Ecchymosed'*.

•

By Order of the Board of Health:
Citizens to forego intercourse with smugglers.
Sick-houses instituted. Tainted dwellings
fumed and limed. The Cavalry as quarantine.

Nurses to forego intercourse with others.
A druggist to each quarter of the city.
Commerce banned between infected towns.
Scavenging on weekly rosters. Piggeries abolished.

Burials to the north side of the Meadow.
Burning and burial of clothing and beds
in Shilhay, St James and Pester Lane –
antient plague and pest-hus for the needy.

Soup tickets to the poor.
Orders for the use of troops / police.

•

Items payd: for Beeswax corks to plug the Diarrhoea;
for Carminatives and Ammonia.

Items pending: for Lime Water, Milk and Laudanum;
for Calomel, Brandy and Opium.

Items irrecoverable: two Poultices and trial Venesection;
two treatments (failed) of friction to the skin.

•

Female, thirty years of age.
A pauper from Gladstone Road Workhouse.
Admitted to quarantine, August fifteenth.
Pulse weak, lips blue, her features much depressed.

Skin cold and clammy. Cramps, emaciation.
Abnormal smell. Intelligence entire.
Vomiting and purging now profuse.
Jactitation. Diarrhoea.

Ordered: One Mustard Emetic.
Water bottles placed upon the soles.
Water for regular drinking
XV grana per hora Calomel.

Refuses to take medicine. A vein opened up,
though blood would but emerge in single drops.

•

It was a sombre morning in the meadow
when the congregation gathered by the graves.
The bulky crowd extended through the gateway
standing in the streets beneath the crosses
set in place to ward away disease.

Respectfully they trailed their reverend father,
who prayed the corpses down the grassy path.
But this that stopped them in their mournful tracks…
the digger and his team of burly men
carrying the coffins underhand.

Why won't you carry caskets as you should?
they asked. To which the gravesman said:
I am just a digger and I must make ends meet.
What pestilence may rain on me by carting
caskets high… what of me, my wife and kids?

The angry crowd replied: *Isn't your faith*
worth more than what you earn? and, pressing on,
their anger spilled into the streets at Southernhay.
What is this bestial burial, meted to our dead?
Is Our Lord no longer present to these bodies?

At this the digger stood his ground
and insults streamed like rapids on the Exe:
You Diddiko, Dipper, you cheating old Duffer,
you rookery Magsman, you Mumper, you Muck Snipe…
you'll get a right Dewskitch, we'll do you right down!

And the angry rabble bore the digger down,
and carried him *hallooing* all the way
to dump him in the Gate House, his voice dying,
the way that a bird's song is drowned
by a sudden downpour of morning rain.

•

16th. 9. A.M. Has passed a very restless night,
afraid to drink lest medicines within.
No motion since yesterday morning,
continues vomiting.

17th. 9. A.M. Has passed a better night.
Pulse perceptible, appendages cold,
yet some degree of warmth
upon the forehead.

6. P.M. Tongue covered with a brownish fur.
Skin cool but dry like cloth.
Vomiting and purging both abated.

To take a little mutton broth.
19th. 10. A.M. Slight stupor. *Venae Sectio* –
black blood with a few spots of buff.

•

Down to the waterworks over Exe Lane,
down to the river for daily supplies.
    Sing: Water from the wealthy, private well.
    Water from the public conduit.
    Water from the public pump…
    And bucket rations to the poor!

My horse, she once was fatter than my barrels.
But now she's as thin as the spokes of my wheels.
    Sing: Water from the wealthy, private well.
    Water from the public conduit.
    Water from the public pump…
    And bucket rations to the poor!

The wells shut tight; new pumps in place.
The silent streets twice-watered every day.
    Sing: Water from the wealthy, private well.
    Water from the public conduit.
    Water from the public pump…
    And bucket rations to the poor!

•

20th. 10. A.M. *fiat pilula*
quarta quaque hora sumenda:
Cupri Sulphatis, gr. ¼
Pulveris Opii, gr. ¼

Has passed a good night
free from pain, pulse soft and full.
A quantity of faecular matter
tinged with bile.

2. P. M. Two bilious motions yesterday.
The colliquative diarrhoea decreased.
A great disposition to sleep.

22nd. Gradually coming back to health.
Pergat in usu pilularum.
('Keep taking the pills.')

•

In Bury Fields the bodies lie
upon the grass in summer time.
The picnickers and students know
this is a place you have to go
to let the days slip idly by.

Where dogs chase sticks and children climb,
the squirrels hoard and blackbirds fly
at liberty before the snows
hide Bury Fields.

And deep beneath, where no one's eye
can penetrate, the bare bones cry:
'We are the Dead – where you now go
we also lived, saw sunsets glow…
sumus cholera perpessae,   *('We are the cholera dead')*
in Bury Fields.'

f i n

The Unnameable Taxonomy

> 'By seeking euphemisms for the WC, we try to deny its existence'.
> —The Water Closet, *Roy Palmer*

> after 'The Names of the Hare', translated from the Middle English by Seamus Heaney

When man or woman, boy or girl
has to answer nature's call
it may go well if you repeat
this litany upon the seat,
with devotion and sincerity:
'The Unnameable Taxonomy'.

Call it…
Going to the House of Ease,
the House of Office, the WC,
the Thinking Room, the Bog, the Loo,
the Fortress Of Your Solitude,
the Boghouse, Jakes, the plain Privie,
the Washroom, or the Lavatory,
the Ladies, Gents, the Smallest Room,
the John, the Can, the Powder Room,
the Outhouse, Restroom, House of Honour,
the House of Morning, the Throne, the Crapper,
the *Garde robe. Necessarium.*
The Pot, the Potty, and the Hole,
the Vladimir. Latrine. The Bowl.

Call it…
Seeing A Man About a Horse,

Disposing Of Your Hazardous Waste,
Dropping the Kids Off at the Pool,
An Evening at the Superbowl,
Having the daily A.M. BM,
Exorcising All Your Demons,
Shooting Out a Game of Craps,
Dropping Anchor, Checking the Pipes,
Catching-up on Some Piled-up Reading,
Evacuating the Crowded Building.

Call it…
Room 101, or Number Two,
Auditing Assets, Doing the Do.
Taking Some Weight Off Your Troubled Mind,
Seeing How Things Turn Out Behind,
Paying The Band, Feeding the Fish,
Call it Making a Special Wish.

Call it…
Bombing the Bowl, Growing a Tail.
Dropping a Biscuit in the Pail,
Planting Corn, Doing the Dog,
Worshipping the Water Gods.
It's Balancing the Daily Budget,
Blowing on the Morning Trumpet,
Putting All Your Thoughts on Paper,
Sparking-up the Ring of Fire…

And when you have intoned this prayer
then you might much better fare.
Unnameable, goodbye to you,
god guide you to a how-d'ye-do
with earth and what the whole world knows:
now, visit the garden and pluck a rose.

The Broad Street Pump

It's summer in the Golden Square.
Crank the lever and watch it pour
five hundred ruined souls, or more.

The G7 Aid Budget
The Bristol Stool Chart, 1997

1: Separate hard lumps, like nuts. Hard to pass.
2: Sausage-shaped, but lumpy.
3: Like a sausage, but cracked on the surface.
4: Like a sausage or snake. Smooth and soft.
5: Soft blobs with clear-cut edges.
6: Fluffy pieces with ragged edges. Mushy.
7: Watery, no solid pieces. Entirely liquid.

The Flying Toilets of Kibera

Kibera is the largest slum in Nairobi, Kenya, and the largest urban slum in Africa. The names in each verse are popular names for Kenyan children, with their meanings.

Because the politicians can't discuss
toilets, for fear of breaking taboo,
Afiyah (Swahili, 'well-being, health')
launches hers beyond Kibera's walls.

Because the bureaucrat believes
the settlement must be 'illegal',
Kanja (Sanskrit, 'water born')
slings his to the reservoir's edge.

As plastic bags rain from the sky
Nafula (African, 'born in the rain')
washes his face in the tainted tank.

You choose, Samira: either use the bag,
or squat outside in the perilous night –
(Arabic, meaning 'pleasurable place').

Note

Watersong begins with the first of the great cholera epidemics of 19th Century England. Focussing on the poet's home city of Exeter, the poems interlace select details from Exeter's 1832 cholera outbreak, in which over 400 people died, with imagined narratives of the epidemic, and other related episodes in the city, factual and invented. The main source of details for the 1832 Exeter cholera outbreak remains Dr Thomas Shapter's book *The Cholera in Exeter* (1849), to which these poems owe a debt.

A number of additional poems deal with contemporary issues of sanitation and water. Globally, some 2,000 children under five still die every day from diarrhoeal diseases. Of these, 1,800 deaths are linked to water, sanitation and hygiene.

CPSIA information can be obtained
at www.ICGtesting.com
Printed in the USA
BVHW030814070619
550445BV00001B/34/P